Smoke Jumpers

By Jim Gigliotti

www.childsworld.com

Published in the United States of America by The Child's World®
P.O. Box 326 • Chanhassen, MN 55317-0326
800-599-READ • www.childsworld.com

Thanks to Rick Rataj for his help in preparing this book.—J. G.

ACKNOWLEDGMENTS

The Child's World®: Mary Berendes, Publishing Director

Produced by Shoreline Publishing Group LLC
President / Editorial Director: James Buckley, Jr.
Designer: Tom Carling, carlingdesign.com
Cover Art: Slimfilms
Copy Editor: Beth Adelman

Photo Credits
All photos by Mike McMillan/Spotfire Images, except the
following—7, 21 courtesy Rick Rataj.

LIBRARY OF CONGRESS CATALOGING-IN-PUBLICATION DATA

Gigliotti, Jim.
  Smoke jumpers / by Jim Gigliotti.
    p. cm. — (Boys rock!)
  Includes bibliographical references and index.
  ISBN 1-59296-735-3 (library bound : alk. paper)
 1. Smokejumpers—Juvenile literature. 2. Wildfire fighters—
Juvenile literature. I. Title. II. Series.
  SD421.23.G54 2006
  634.9'618—dc22
                        2006001638

CONTENTS

ONE-OF-A-KIND Job!

Rick Rataj stands in the open doorway of an airplane. He is flying high above a forest where a fire is raging. Most people would be worried, but Rick is ready to go to work.

Rick is a smoke jumper—a special kind of firefighter who uses a **parachute** to jump into the forest to fight fires. Without smoke jumpers, it might take

many hours—even days—to reach a **remote** fire. The smoke jumpers' speed can mean saving hundreds of **acres** of forest. Getting there fast also saves property, animals, and sometimes even people.

Look out below! A smoke jumper aims his chute toward the fire zone.

Smoke jumpers can steer their parachutes by pulling on special cords.

To be a smoke jumper, you need to have basic firefighting skills as well as experience fighting **wildfires**. You also need to be an expert parachutist and be in peak physical and mental condition. The work is difficult and long. Smoke jumpers face demanding workdays that can last up to 16 hours.

In this daring job, you need a sense of adventure and excitement, too.

"I learned the excitement of jumping out of planes in the military," Rick says. "I knew it was fun to jump out of an airplane, so I was fired up to go into smoke jumping."

Experience Counts

Rick Rataj, a smoke jumper for six years, works from the station in Redding, California. Many jumpers work all summer and then have the winter off, when fires are less likely. Rick goes on 20 to 25 jumps a year.

Smoke jumpers are a select group of men and women. There are only about 400 in the United States—and only about 20 new jumpers are hired each year.

This word comes from knitting. The stitches in a knitted item are very close together.

Because they are few in number, and because it is such a difficult and dangerous job, smoke jumpers are a **close-knit** group. When they are not in the forest fighting fires, they are back at the base station helping each other out. Everyone has different responsibilities.

Some jumpers repair
parachutes, while others
pack boxes of food and
water or chainsaws and gas.
These boxes will be ready for
the next fire call.

*Women can
be smoke
jumpers, too.*

Smoke jumpers practice landings in swimming pools.

All smoke jumpers have to pass a physical test before they are hired. They have to pass it again every spring. Among the tests: run a mile and a half (2 km) in less than 11 minutes.

Candidates have to do a series of 7 pull-ups, 25 push-ups, and 45 sit-ups. They must also jog a three-mile (5 km) course in less than 45 minutes—all while carrying a 45-pound (20 kg) pack. It's even harder than it sounds!

Smoke jumpers need to stay in excellent physical shape. Each day after **roll call**, jumpers work out for 90 minutes. They can run, swim, lift weights, or bike. Smoke jumpers' hard work in the gym pays off with safe work in the field.

Why all the hard work? Smoke jumpers need their strength for long hours, lots of hiking, and lots of hard work.

2

TOOLS OF THE
Trade

The parachute is the main piece of equipment that separates a smoke jumper from other firefighters.

Before every jump, the smoke jumpers inspect their parachutes for rips or tears. Then the parachutes are refolded and repacked. An inspector signs off on them, and they are ready for the next jump. All jumpers carry a main parachute on their back and a smaller, backup parachute in the front. Good preparation makes for safe jumping.

OPPOSITE PAGE

Inspectors check out a smoke-jumper's parachute before every jump.

The tan jumpsuit this firefighter wears helps keep him safe in the air and when he lands.

The suit is flame-retardant, which means it is hard to burn. The suit will eventually catch fire, but it can protect the wearer from fire and heat for a short time.

Smoke jumpers wear **flame-retardant** jumpsuits. The pants have pockets for items such as a 150-foot (46-m) "letdown rope," used when a jumper gets stuck in a tree.

The helmet has wire **mesh** over the face to keep the jumper from getting scraped by branches or rocks. A jumper's thick gloves offer extra protection, too.

Smoke jumpers can quickly open and climb into the fire shelter for a few moments of safety.

One item every jumper carries (but hopes never to need) is a fire shelter. It's a small, shiny, silver tent. When surrounded by fire, the jumper can crawl into this tent. The silver material protects the jumper from the intense heat.

The heavy boxes of gear and supplies need several parachutes to be dropped safely.

Smoke jumpers need more than they can carry with them, however. After dropping the jumpers, the airplane returns and drops boxes attached to big parachutes. The boxes, which are full of gear, drift down to the smoke jumpers.

These are the boxes the jumpers packed during their time at the base. Some of the boxes contain canned food, snacks, and water to give the jumpers energy during the hours—or days—ahead.

Other boxes have the heavy-duty fire-fighting equipment the jumpers need to do their job. They'll use shovels, chainsaws, picks, axes, and a special tool for fighting forest fires called a **pulaski**.

After removing their jumpsuits, smoke jumpers unpack their gear and get ready to move out to the fire.

The pulaski (below) is a two-in-one tool for both chopping and making trenches. It is one of the smoke jumper's most useful tools. The pulaski's head has an axe on one side and a hoe on the other, which helps when digging trenches. The tool is named for Edward Pulaski, a ranger who invented it in the early 1900s.

Smoke jumpers and pulaskis in action! Digging a trench around a fire gives it nothing to burn and helps put out the fire.

Chainsaws and shovels help clear away brush and trees. Another one-of-a-kind tool is a **drip torch,** which is used to start **backfires**.

Why start a fire? By creating this kind of small, controlled fire, the smoke jumper can help put out the main fire. That's because fire usually can't burn over an area that has already been burned.

Fire Call!

A loud horn sounds at the base station. Someone has spotted a fire in the forest! It's time for the smoke jumpers to move into action.

All the jumpers head to their lockers and put on their gear as quickly as possible. They grab their parachutes and a personal-gear bag that includes their fire shelter, snacks, and maybe some extra socks.

Before boarding the plane that will take them to the **drop spot,** each jumper works with a "buddy" to check each other's equipment one more time. Then they're good to go!

Smoke jumpers don't use fancy passenger jets. Instead, they use smaller propeller planes.

A small fire, perhaps one tree that has been struck by lightning, might need only two or three jumpers. But a larger fire, maybe a 10-acre (4 ha) blaze, might take eight to 10 jumpers. Once the jumpers are aboard the plane, they head to a clear jump spot. Jumpers are only dropped into safe areas.

A canopy is a protective covering over something. In the forest, it's formed by the tops of all the trees, which shelter the area below.

"We always jump to a clear spot, so we can be sure we're safe," Rick says. "You can almost always find a clear area or an opening in the **forest canopy.**

"We look for a meadow, a
log deck, a road . . . anything
big enough for us to jump
safely in there."

*When the
plane nears the
drop spot, the
jumpers line
up at the door,
ready to make
their jumps.*

No turning back! A smoke jumper leaps out of the plane.

A crew member drops streamers of colored paper out of the plane to see which way the wind is blowing. Then, when the pilot gives the all-clear signal, the jumpers leap out the door!

The jumpers drift down toward the drop zone, landing softly (they hope!). Then they gather their parachutes. They agree on a "safety zone," where they'll meet in case of emergency.

They examine the area and check their **compasses**. They get final instructions from their crew leader.

"Then it's time for the not-so-fancy part of the job," Rick says. It's time to grab a chainsaw and a pulaski and get to work!

Smoke jumpers might have to hike a long distance from their drop zone to get to the fire itself.

After hiking to the fire, the jumpers' first order of business is creating a fire line. That's a cleared strip around the fire, like a trail, to rob the fire of the fuel that it needs to burn. Jumpers use their chainsaws, shovels, and other equipment to clear away brush or trees— anything that the fire can use as fuel.

"Anchor, Flank, and Pinch"

That's the three-part plan that smoke jumpers use to put out a forest fire. "Anchor the back of the fire, flank [go to the sides of] the fire, then pinch the head," Rick says.

The jumpers dig down to the soil, which does not burn. For small fires, the fire line might be only a couple of feet wide. For big fires, it might be several yards across.

When water hoses can be brought in, smoke jumpers can really tackle a fire.

After the blaze is contained with a fire line, the smoke jumpers begin "mop-up" work to put the fire out completely. To do this, they'll mix and stir the dirt with water to cool the ashes down.

Once the fire is totally out, it's time for the jumpers to get on their hands and knees. They feel the fire area to make sure there's no heat left on the ground.

It's dirty work, but smoke jumpers do the job because they love it!

The fire is out! The smoke jumpers' job is done. Their hard work and training have paid off. Now it's time to pack up and head back to the base—and get ready for the next fire call.

GLOSSARY

acres a unit of measure for large areas of land (1 acre = 43,560 square feet or 4,047 square meters)

backfires fires started on purpose to burn away fuel so a forest fire can't advance

close-knit having a very tight relationship with one another

compasses devices used to tell direction, with a magnetic needle that always points north

drip torch a tool that drips fuel and flame to start backfires and other carefully controlled outdoor fires

drop spot the safe area where the smoke jumpers are supposed to land

flame-retardant made of a material that resists fire and heat for a short time

forest canopy the high covering formed by the meeting of treetops above a forest

mesh a net made of woven wires or threads with spaces in between

parachute a piece of light, strong cloth that lets a person or an object float safely to the ground from an airplane

pulaski a fire-fighting tool with an axe and a hoe

remote far away from people or buildings

roll call a way of taking attendance

FIND OUT MORE

BOOKS

Fire Line
by Michael Thoele
(Fulcrum Publishing, Golden, CO) 1995
Information about all types of forest firefighters, including smoke jumpers.

Smokejumpers
by Elaine Landau
(The Millbrook Press, Brookfield, CT) 2002
Includes information on how smoke jumpers are trained and takes readers along on a fire fight.

Smokejumpers: Life Fighting Fires
by Mark Beyer
(Rosen Publishing Group, New York) 2001
Photos and inside stories of life as a smoke jumper.

WEB SITES

Visit our home page for lots of links about smoke jumpers:
www.childsworld.com/links

Note to Parents, Teachers, and Librarians: We routinely check our Web links to make sure they're safe, active sites—so encourage your readers to check them out!

INDEX

JIM GIGLIOTTI is a writer who lives in southern California with his wife and two children. He has written more than a dozen books for young people and adults, including *Stadium Stories: USC Trojans* and *Watching Football* (with former NFL star Daryl Johnston).